A BOOK OF SWEETHEARTS

A BOOK OF SWEETHEARTS

PICTURES BY
FAMOUS
AMERICAN ARTISTS

DECORATIONS BY
WILL JENKINS

"Be good Sweetheart and
let who will be clever."

Gramercy Books
New York

This 2001 edition is published by Gramercy Books™, an imprint of Random House Value Publishing, Inc., 280 Park Avenue, New York, NY 10017.

Gramercy Books™ and design are trademarks of Random House Value Publishing, Inc.

Random House
New York • Toronto • London • Sydney • Auckland
http://www.randomhouse.com/

Printed in Hong Kong

Library of Congress Cataloging-in-Publication Data

A book of sweethearts : pictures by famous American artists / decorations by Will Jenkins.
        p. cm.
  Originally published: Indianapolis : Bobbs-Merrill, 1908.
  ISBN 0-517-16270-9
    1. Women in art. 2. Love in art. 3. Painting, American. 4. Painting, Modern--19th century—United States. 5. Painting, Modern—20th century—United States. I. Jenkins, Will.

ND1460.W65 B66 2001
759.13—dc21

                                                                00-057674

8 7 6 5 4 3 2

DEDICATION

I have known many,
Liked a few,
Loved one—
Here's to you!

THE sweetest flower that blows
        I give you as we part;
For you it is a rose;
        For me it is my heart.

The fragrance it exhales
        (Ah, if you only knew!)
Which but in dying fails,
        It is my love of you.

The sweetest flower that grows
        I give you as we part;
You think it but a rose;
        Ah, me! it is my heart.

HERE'S to the girl I love—God bless her!
Here's to her eyes that tender shine!
Here's to the lips that melt on mine!
To the shining tresses, uncontrolled,
That fall on her neck like tendrils of gold;
To her little mouth and dainty chin;
To the little dimples, out and in!—

                Here's to the girl I love—
                        God bless her!

ABOUT my Darling's lovely eyes
I've made no end of verses;
About her precious little mouth,
Songs, which each voice rehearses—

About my Darling's little cheek,
I wrote a splendid sonnet;
And,—if she only had a heart,
I'd write an ode upon it.

HERE'S to the gladness of her gladness
when she's glad!
Here's to the sadness of her sadness
when she's sad!
But the gladness of her gladness
And the sadness of her sadness
Are not in it with her madness
when she's mad!

THEY may talk of love in a cottage,
  And bowers of trellised vine,
Of nature bewitchingly simple,
  And milkmaids half divine.

BUT give me a sly flirtation
  By the light of a chandelier—
With music to play in the pauses,
  And nobody very near.

HER lips were so near
  That—what else could I do?

    You'll be angry, I fear,
      But her lips were so near—

Well, I can't make it clear
  Or explain it to you,

    But—her lips were so near,
      That—what else could I do?

TRUE love is at home on a carpet,
            And mightily likes his ease,—
And true love has an eye for a dinner
            And starves beneath shady trees.

His wing is the fan of a lady,
  His foot's an invisible thing,
And his arrow is tipp'd with a jewel,
  And shot from a silver string.

UNLESS you can think, when the song is done,
No other is soft in the rhythm;

Unless you can feel, when left by one
That all men else go with him—

Unless you can know when unpraised by his breath
That your beauty itself wants proving;
Unless you can swear—"For life, for death!"
Oh, fear to call it loving!

ROSE kissed me today,
Will she kiss me tomorrow?
Let it be as it may,
Rose kissed me today.

But the pleasure gives way
To a savour of sorrow.
Rose kissed me today—
Will she kiss me tomorrow?

THEY talk about a woman's sphere as
                though it had a limit.—
There's not a place in earth or heaven,
There's not a task to mankind given,
There's not a blessing or a woe,

    There's not a whispered yes or no,
    There's not a life or birth
    That has a feather's weight of worth,
        Without a woman in it.

OH! talk not to me of a name
                great in story,
The days of our youth are the days
                of our glory;
And the myrtle and ivy
        of sweet one-and-twenty
Are worth all your laurels,
        though ever so plenty!

YOU may run the whole gamut
of color and shade,
A pretty girl, however you dress her,
Is the prettiest thing that was ever made;
And the last one is always the prettiest.
Bless her!

THE wheat bends down
With its golden crown,
And it's ho! for the lass that
loves me!
It's a brief, bright way
To the parson's town,
Then it's ho! for the lass that
loves me!

For her eyes are bright
As the twinklin' light
Of the stars o'er the wheat
fields shinin',
An' never I roam
But they light me home
Where the lass for me is
pinin'.

Let the golden crown
Of the wheat bend down—
It's all for the lass that loves me!
The parson's town
An' the weddin' gown,
An' the lips of the lass that
loves me!

ONE kiss from all others prevents me,
  And sets all my pulses astir,
And burns on my lips and torments me:
  'Tis the kiss that I fain would give her.

    One kiss from all others requites me,
      Although it is never to be,
    And sweetens my dreams and invites me:
      'Tis the kiss that she dare not give me.

HE said when first he saw me,
  Life seemed at once divine,
Each night he dreamed of angels,
  And every face was mine;

Sometimes a voice in sleeping
  Would all his hopes forbid;
And then he'd waken weeping
  Do you really think he did?

THOU art so very sweet and fair,
    With such a heaven in thine eyes,
It almost seems an overcare
    To ask them to be good or wise.

As if a little bird were blam'd
    Because its song unthinking flows;
As if a rose should be asham'd
    Of being nothing but a rose.

SEE the mountains kiss high heaven,
    And the waves clasp one another;
No sister flower would be forgiven
    If it disdained its brother;

And the sunlight clasps the earth,
    And the moonbeams kiss the sea;
What are all these kissings worth,
    If thou kiss not me?

THERE'S a little Saxon proverb
    That goes very much like this,
That a man is half in Heaven
When he wants a woman's kiss—

        But there's danger in delaying,
        For the sweetness may forsake it,
        So I ask you, tasteful lover,
        If you wish one, why not take it?

SHE wears a rose in her hair.
　　At the twilight's dreamy close
Her face is fair, <u>how</u> fair
　　Under the rose!

I steal like a shadow there,
　　As she sits in rapt repose,
And whisper my loving prayer
　　Under the rose!

She takes the rose from her hair,
　　And her color comes and goes;
And I—a lover will dare
　　Under the rose!

MAY in the woods and in my heart
　　And we beside the river;
　　　　　King Love between us flying
　　　　　　Said, "Children, love forever."

I heard him, and I thought she heard,
　　Her lips began to quiver,
And so I shyly kissed her;
　　Love laughed along the river.

THOUGH in this rapid transit age
    To shorten all things is the rage;

        Though novel, sermon, poem and play
        Grow briefer with each hurrying day,—

One bulwark still defies endeavor—
A kiss is just as long as ever.

JENNY kissed me when we met,
    Jumping from the chair she sat in;
Time, you thief! who love to get
    Sweets into your list, put that in.
Say I'm weary, say I'm sad;
    Say that health and wealth have
        missed me;
Say I'm growing old, but add—
        Jenny kissed me!

HE kissed me—and I know 'twas wrong,
    For he was neither kith nor kin,
Need one do penance very long
    For such a tiny little sin?

He pressed my hand—that wasn't right!
    Why <u>will</u> men have such wicked ways?
It wasn't for a minute, quite,
    But in it there were days and days!

There's mischief in the moon, I know,
    I'm positive I saw her wink
When I requested him to go;
    I meant it, too, I almost think.

But, after all, I'm not to blame,
    He took the kiss, I do think men
Are quite without the sense of shame!
    I wonder when he'll come again.

I DARE not ask a kiss;
    I dare not beg a smile;
Lest having that or this,
    I might grow proud the while.

    No, no, the utmost share
        Of my desires shall be,
    Only to kiss that air
        That lately kissèd thee.

TO my sweetheart—
        she is not a Goddess,

An angel, a lily or a pearl,
She's just that which is sweetest.
        Completest and neatest,

A dear little, queer little,
                Sweet little girl.

"HERE'S to the prettiest,
            Here's to the wittiest,
        Here's to the truest of all who are true;

Here's to the neatest one,
Here's to the sweetest one,
Here's to them all in one—
        Here's to you!"

WHO has not looked upon her brow
　　Has never dreamed of perfect bliss;
But once to see her is to know
　　What beauty, what perfection, is.

　　Her charms are of the growth of heaven,
　　　　She decks the night with hues of day:
　　Blest are the eyes to which 'tis given
　　　　On her to gaze the soul away!

HERE'S to woman, the
　　source of all our bliss;
There's a foretaste of heaven
　　in her kiss;
But from the queen upon her
　　throne to the maiden
　　in her dairy,
They are all alike, in one
　　respect—contrary!

Do you remember when you heard
My lips breathe love's first faltering word?
   You do, sweet—don't you?
When, having wandered all the day,
Linked arm in arm I dared to say,
   You'll love me—won't you?

And when you blushed, and could not speak,
I fondly kissed your glowing cheek;
   Did that affront you?
Oh, surely not; your eye exprest
No wrath, but said, perhaps in jest,
   "You'll love me—won't you?"

I'm sure my eyes replied, "I will;"
And you believe that promise still;
   You do, sweet—don't you?
Yes, yes, when age has made our eyes
Unfit for questions or replies,
   You'll love me—won't you?

IN a world of ceasless changes,
　　　Where all things fade and pine,
Where love, like fancy, ranges
　　　Down many a tangled line,

There are just two hearts worth knowing:
　　　Just two, whose constant glowing
No sign of change is showing,—
　　　Your heart, sweetheart, and mine.

CONFESS, ye volunteers,
　　Lieutenant and Ensign,
　And Captain of the line,
　　As bold as Roman—

Confess, ye grenadiers,
　However strong and tall,
The Conqueror of you all
　　Is Woman, Woman!

NO corselet is so proof
　But through it from her bow
　　　　The shafts that she can throw
　　　Will pierce and rankle.

No champion e'er so tough
　But's in the struggle thrown,
And tripp'd and trodden down
　　By her slim ankle.

SHE is not fair to outward view
    As many maidens be;

            Her loveliness I never knew
            Until she smiled on me.

      O then I saw her eye was bright,
      A well of love, a spring of light.

BUT now her looks are coy
    and cold,
    To mine they ne'er reply,

And yet I cease not to behold
    The love-light in her eye:

Her very frowns are fairer far
Than smiles of other maidens are.

I LOVE thee—I love thee!
    Is ever on my tongue.
In all my proudest poesy
    That chorus still is sung.

    It is the verdict of my eyes
        Amidst the gay and young:
    I love thee—I love thee!
        A thousand maids among.

I love thee—I love thee!
    Thy bright and hazel glance,
The mellow lute upon those lips,
    Whose tender tones entrance.

    But most dear heart of hearts, thy proofs,
        That still these words enhance!
    I love thee—I love thee!
        Whatever be my chance.

THE clover blossoms kiss
        her feet,
    She is so sweet,
While I who may not kiss
        her hand
Bless all the wild flowers in
        the land.

Soft sunshine falls across
        her breast,
    She is so blest,
I'm jealous of its arms
        of gold;
Oh, that these arms her
        form might hold!

Gently the breezes kiss her hair,
        She is so fair!

Let flowers and sun and breeze go by,
O dearest! Love me or I die.

YOUR whim is for frolic
and fashion,
Your taste is for letters
and art: —

This rhyme is the
commonplace passion
That glows in a fond
woman's heart;

Lay it by in some sacred
deposit
For relics, — we all have a
few!

Love, some day they'll print
it, because it
Was written
to you.

I SEEM, in the midst of the crowd,
    The lightest of all;
        My laughter rings cheery and loud
        In banquet and ball.

My lip hath its smiles and its sneers,
    For all men to see;
But my soul, and my truth, and my tears
    Are for thee, are for thee!

A ROUND me they flatter and fawn—
    The young and the old,
The fairest are ready to pawn
    Their hearts for my gold.

They sue me—I laugh as I spurn
    The slaves at my knee;
But in faith and in fondness I turn
    Unto thee, unto thee!

O SWEETHEARTS, for the love you bear to men, like as much of this book as pleases you: O men, for the love you bear to sweethearts, may the book be fruitful to you and bountifully please.